ELTON W,

The Pottery of Sir Edmund Elton

by

Malcolm Haslam

Fig. 1. Sir Edmund Elton c. 1885.

DEDICATORY

In dedicating this study to the memory of the eminent historian of technology Sir Arthur Elton, the tenth baronet, who admired his grandfather's pottery for both its artistic and its technical merits, I would like at the same time to thank Lady Elton for bearing so patiently all the inconvenience to which I have put her, for entertaining me so hospitably, and for allowing me access to the comprehensive archives on all aspects of Elton ware, which she and Sir Arthur so diligently assembled. Thankyou.

Malcolm Haslam
April 1989.

ACKNOWLEDGEMENTS

For some years collectors have been looking for a monograph on Elton ware and we are pleased to launch this book at Libertys to coincide with an exhibition of Elton Pottery.

We would like to thank Lady Elton for her support with this project and we are very grateful to the collectors whose pots have been made available for us to study and photograph, and who wish to remain anonymous. The author is indebted to John Bartlett for sharing his extensive knowledge of Elton pottery and we thank the Rev. R. Ghest for allowing us to photograph in Tickenham Church.

Print Design and Reproduction by Flaydemouse, Yeovil, England.
Photography by Mike Bruce at Gate Studios.
Cover photography by Matthew Donaldson.

© 1989 Richard Dennis and Malcolm Haslam

Published and distributed by Richard Dennis, Shepton Beauchamp, Ilminster, Somerset TA19 0JT, England.

ISBN 0 903685 25 6

Illustration on front cover: Crackled lustre pots. Private collection.
Illustration on back cover: Slipware. Private collection.

CONTENTS

Fig. 2. Agnes Mary Elton, c. 1870.

Fig. 3. The servants at Clevedon Court, c. 1870.

Chapter 1

The Early Years

There are various accounts of how and when Edmund Elton (fig. 1) started trying to make pottery. None is very clear, nor are they entirely consistent. Naturally, the most authoritative must be that given by Sir Edmund himself, when he addressed the Somersetshire Archaeological and Natural History Society in 1910. But his narrative presents little more than the bare bones, and in order to add some flesh it is necessary to turn to some secondary sources as well.

In December 1879 Elton, aged thirty three, went to a local brickworks to investigate the manufacture of tiles. While watching the men at work, he conceived the idea of making ceramic pictures, composed of differently coloured clays. He ordered some tiles, dry but unfired, to be sent to his home, Firwood, at Clevedon in Somerset. There he created a half-length portrait of Sir Philip Sidney the Elizabethan poet by cutting up the slabs of clay of three different colours, and arranging the pieces. The portrait was a copy of an original in stained glass at Clevedon Court, the Elton family seat. He then made some modifications to an old greenhouse furnace, in the hope it would serve as a kiln. He fired his clay picture in it, but, in his own words, 'the result, as may be expected was a total failure'.

He tried to build a proper kiln, but after at least two failures he decided to seek professional advice. He visited Pountney's Victoria Pottery in Bristol, and there the manager allowed him to examine and measure a small enamelling kiln. Pountney's also provided him with some glaze and raw colours. Back at Clevedon, with the help of a bricklayer, he built a replica of the kiln he had seen at Bristol and at last began to achieve 'some fairly good results'. The first successful piece was a three-quarter length figure of St Stephen, which he described as a 'mosaic panel in drab, black and yellow, on a bluish-green dispersed ground'. Subsequent firings, however, were not so satisfactory, and more than once the kiln had to be pulled down and rebuilt.

Edmund Elton soon decided to abandon tile pictures, and to start making art pottery. He considered coiling or casting his pots but eventually employed a flowerpot-maker to throw for him. 'I used to stand by,' he recalled thirty years later, 'as the pieces grew under the thrower's hand, and say, "Stop now, bulge out there, draw in here", and so on, till something satisfactory appeared.' Various decorative techniques were attempted, including underglaze painting; finally he decided to make a slip-decorated ware.

'In the early part of 1881,' according to Sir Edmund, problems were caused by limestone in the clay body. Professor A. H. Church,

Elton's friend and mentor, writing in *The Portfolio* towards the end of 1882, implied that this difficulty arose much earlier. Although some of Elton's early pieces were successful, Church averred, 'they contained fragments of limestone burnt into quick lime in the kiln; these fragments afterwards broke up the glaze by their expansion on gradually becoming slaked on exposure to the air'. The trouble was overcome by preparing the clay body in a slip-kiln where, presumably, the limestone was burnt off.

From June 12th, 1880, Elton was on holiday in Scotland for about a month. On his return he embarked on a long series of trial firings with very mixed results. He tried burning various fuels in the kiln – coke, coal and wood – to eliminate the sulphur which for a time ruined most of the ware. He tried salt-glazing, but with no success. 'The difficulties and disappointments encountered were so many,' wrote Church, 'that for four months not a single satisfactory specimen was drawn from the kiln.' The coloured slips with which the pottery was decorated tended at first to crack and peel away from the body of the ware. The presence of oxide of iron dulled many of the colours. But Elton persevered. Apart from frequent trial firings, which were almost daily at some stages, he was building much of his own equipment as it was required. 'With the aid of the estate carpenter and the local blacksmith' a kick-wheel was constructed. Elton practised throwing, and he was soon proficient enough to dispense with the

Fig. 5 Right. Clevedon Court, south front, c. 1885.

services of the flowerpot-maker.

George Masters, one of the men employed in the gardens at Clevedon Court, watched the would-be potter at work and his interest was aroused. He hurried through his chores so that he could spend more time at the sheds where the pottery was situated. Elton often called on him for assistance and soon invited the eighteen-year old to join him full time. Masters learnt to throw, and to Elton's delight he 'more and more faithfully translated my ideas'.

Gradually the successes overhauled the failures, although disasters would always continue to occur throughout the forty years of the pottery's operation. By March, 1881, Edmund Elton and George Masters were producing pottery in sufficient quantity – and of adequate quality – to be able to supply it to retailers in Bristol and London. To have arrived at this position hardly more than fifteen months after Elton had first considered making pottery, was an enormous achievement. In those days, neither equipment nor materials were supplied with printed instructions, and there were no practical manuals. It was impossible to enrol in pottery classes; there were none. Although it has to be remembered that there were only the mildest financial constraints on Elton's endeavour, he was clearly a man of great ability. He must have had a considerable knowledge of chemistry, physics and mechanics. He obviously possessed an abundance of practicality and more than a modicum of perseverance. In addition he displayed an estimable artistic talent and great good taste. Some account should be given of such a man's upbringing.

Edmund Harry Elton was born on May 3rd, 1846, in Clifton near Bristol. There were complications at the birth and his mother, Lucy Maria, died bearing him. Some blame was attached to his father, Edward William Elton, who had apparently been less attentive

Fig. 6 Left. George Masters decorating c. 1890.

Fig. 7 Right. Page from 'Pottery Account' kept by Edmund Elton from March 29th, 1881.

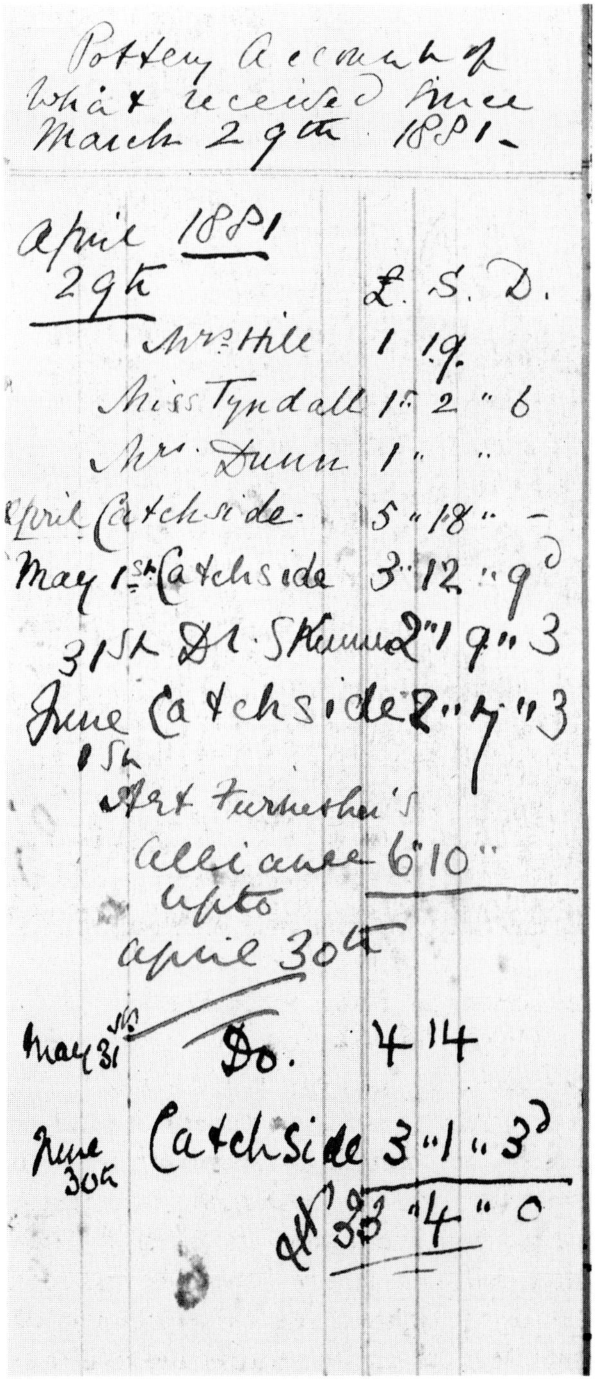

Pottery Account of
What received since
March 29th 1881.

April 1881
29th £. S. D.
Mrs Hill 1 19.
Miss Tyndall 1" 2 " 6
Mrs Dunn 1 "
April Catchside 5 " 18 " –
May 1st Catchside 3" 12 " 9d
31st Dr Skinner 2" 19" 3
June 15th Catchside 2" 7 " 3
Art Furnisher's Alliance 6" 10"
up to April 30th
May 31st Do. 4 14
June 30th Catchside 3" 1 " 3d
Do 4" 0

during the critical hours than might have been expected of a good husband. Another cloud hung over the father's reputation; he had abandoned an undistinguished career as an officer in the Royal Navy rather more readily than the regulations allowed. It was decided that Edward, who was quite an accomplished artist, should go and live in Italy, and that his new-born son should be brought up by an uncle and aunt in London. Admiral Samuel Thornton, retired, a director of the Peninsular & Orient shipping line, was approaching fifty. His wife, Emily Elizabeth, was the elder sister of Edmund Elton's deceased mother. They had two children, Percy and Clare, who were only a few years older than their cousin. The Thorntons lived at 12 Upper Gloucester Place, 'not a residence,' wrote Percy Thornton, looking back on it sixty years later, 'which would reach the ideal of Mr Ruskin in a due proportion of colour prevailing around'. In the early eighteen fifties, however, the Thorntons moved to a big house in more rural surroundings at Blackheath.

According to the critic and poet Cosmo Monkhouse, who wrote an account of Elton's pottery in the *Magazine of Art* in 1883, Edmund had 'an early bias towards art, which was not without some slight cultivation'. Emily Thornton was a proficient water-colourist, whose sketches of the Swiss landscape were always to be particularly treasured by her children. Edmund himself would later paint watercolours of the same scenery with considerable skill.

The Thorntons used to spend much time in Brighton at 6 Royal Crescent, the home of Mrs Rice, Emily Thornton's mother and Edmund Elton's grandmother. From the seafront the Admiral used to watch through his telescope the P. & O. liners as they sailed down the Channel bound for India. At Brighton, too, Edmund made an early impact on the senior clergy of the Church of England. Bishop Bagot of Bath and Wells was Mrs Rice's next-door neighbour; he was, according to Percy Thornton, 'a martyr to gout'. He would 'joyfully welcome the children's presence, and then shrink from the strong grasp of the hand which [Edmund Elton] then insisted on giving to all his special friends and associates'. This was not to be Elton's sole contact with the Anglican clergy, as we shall see, nor the last occasion on which he would discomfort a Bishop of Bath and Wells.

The first school which Elton attended was at Brighton. Probably this was Crescent House where Percy Thornton was a pupil from 1850 to 1856. Thornton remembered it as 'an old-fashioned establishment' where standards were maintained by frequent use of the cane. The school was run by Mr Adams and Mr Langtry, 'both . . . useful members of the Sussex County Gentleman's team as bowlers of fair capacity'.

In 1859 double tragedy befell Edmund Elton; both his real and adoptive fathers died. Edward Elton had lived in Florence since 1843. He had married an Italian lady, Clementina, who had borne him two daughters, Minna and Marion, Edmund's stepsisters. Admiral Thornton died, as he might have wished, at sea; he fell overboard from a P. & O. liner in the Bay of Biscay and drowned. Possibly Edmund's being sent away to boarding school the same year was related to the Admiral's death and his widow's distress.

Bradfield College, near Reading, had been founded only ten years before Elton went there. Already some traditions had been established, including the decoration of classrooms with flowers and foliage to celebrate the feast of St Andrew, the school's patron saint. As each class collected its greenery and brought it back along the narrow lanes of the Berkshire countryside, the boys were liable to be ambushed and robbed of their loads by members of a rival form. 'One year,' a former pupil recorded, 'the star of the Junior Classroom was in the ascendant, for it found a magnificent leader of irregulars in Elton.' He won a hurdle race at the school's annual sports, but this seems to have been the extent of any impact that he made on the College during the year he was there.

One of the school's new buildings may have made an impression on Elton. In 1856 the Hall had been built to a design by Gilbert Scott based on a medieval English tithe-barn. The roof was supported by ten squared trunks of elm trees cut from the woods on the estate, and the exposed struts, beams and rafters were of the same origin. The floor was paved

Fig. 8 Right. Family and friends at Clevedon Court 1886. Sir Edmund is seated cross-legged on the top step.

with Minton's encaustic tiles and there was an elaborate neo-gothic fireplace. Carved ornament on the mantelpiece and some medallions in the stained glass windows were designed by Susan Stevens, wife of the College's founder. Of greater importance, however, was the stained glass in the west window, which was designed by Edward Burne-Jones. It was made in 1857 by James Powell & Sons of Whitefriars and was one of Burne-Jone's earliest designs for stained glass. From the same building Elton might well have assimilated a notion of the practical craftsmanship which was to permeate his adult life and lead to his endeavours as a potter. For, above one of the doors to the Hall, there had been placed a clay panel modelled in low relief, depicting the fable of the hare and the tortoise; it was the work of Rev Thomas Stevens, founder of the College, vicar of the parish and lord of the manor. The idea would have been implanted in the young Elton's mind that, if the artistic embellishment of one's environment was an obligation of privilege and property, it was a duty upon which one could oneself be engaged.

Between leaving Bradfield in 1860 and going up to Jesus College, Cambridge, four years later, Elton did not apparently undergo any formal education, though he may well have been privately tutored. At Jesus it was again his athletic prowess which has been recorded, rather than any intellectual accomplishment. In 1864 he won the Larkin Challenge Cup for sculling, and the following year he rowed in the college boat. He read chemistry but went down without taking a degree.

The next and last educational establishment attended by Edmund Elton was the Royal Agricultural College at Cirencester. Here, at last, he received the kind of training which would be useful to him in later life and which would allow him to indulge his natural inclination towards practical science. As well as a chemical laboratory, the College boasted a lathe-room, a carpenter's shop and three forges. Architectural and mechanical drawing was included in the course of instruction. But the greatest boon bestowed on Elton during his time at Cirencester was the friendship and influence of Arthur Herbert Church, F.R.S., who was professor of chemistry at the College.

Fig. 9 Left. Plaque cast from original plaster portrait of Kathleen Elton modelled by Hubert von Herkomer in 1885. Incised on rim 'Reproduced 1905'. Diameter 37.5 cm.

Plate 1 Right. Slipware vases. Height of tallest 49.6 cm.

Church lived in college and his knowledge of, and enthusiasm for, a wide range of topics related to both science and art were easily shared by the students. In turn, he liked to take part in some of their activities. 'For recreation,' he wrote in his *Records & Recollections*, 'I enjoyed greatly accompanying geological and botanical excursions, walks to Sapperton and the Golden Valley, Malmesbury, Tetbury . . . and railway trips to Stroud, Gloucester, Cheltenham, Bath, Bristol . . . It was mainly during these excursions that my collection of Old English Earthenware was formed.' This collection grew to include more than 800 pieces, and Elton had been able to inspect it before 535 of the best examples were destroyed by fire in 1873, when on loan to an exhibiton at the Alexandra Palace. At the time that Elton was a student at Cirencester, Church was just beginning to collect early slipware. Over the years, this class of pottery became one of his favourites, and in 1893 he published a lengthy article in *The Portfolio* on 'Old English Slipware'.

The part which Sir Arthur Church played in the revival of the crafts in Britain during the second half of the nineteenth century was well described in a memoir of him written by Profession A. P. Laurie in the *Transactions of the Chemical Society*, volume 109 (1916):

In the modern scientific period great progress has been made in the application of science to technical processes – a progress which has usually resulted in turning out large quantities of cheap articles with the complete sacrifice of any artistic merit whatever. During the latter half of the nineteenth century the essential inferiority of modern technical processes was begun to be realised, and attempts were being made on the part of men of artistic training – of whom William Morris was the leader – to study minutely the technical processes of the past, and to combine artistic merit and design with fine technical production . . . Of this movement, which is still going on, and is slowly and dimly feeling its way to a different standard of workmanship, and therefore a different standard of life for those engaged in the crafts, Sir Arthur Church may be described as the man of science. His intense appreciation of artistic work of all kinds, his enthusiasm as a collector, and his profound interest in archaeology, led him to apply modern scientific methods to solving the technical problems of the past, and combining in the most interesting way the study of art for art's sake, with the application to it of chemistry.

Church was well qualified to fill the role of scientific adviser to artists and craftsmen. As well as being a brilliant chemist, he was no mean artist, exhibiting landscapes at the Royal Academy on five occasions and at the British Institution on three. This rare combination of talents was recognised by the Royal Academy when, in 1879, he was appointed professor of chemistry at Burlington House.

On July 7th 1868 Edmund Elton married his cousin Agnes, one of Sir Arthur Elton's two daughters (fig. 2). Edmund had first visited Clevedon Court, his family's ancestral home, in 1856 when he was ten years old. Sir Arthur having no sons, Edmund had been since the death of his father in 1859 the heir presumptive to the baronetcy. When Mrs Thornton had died in 1867, Edmund had become, as it were, an orphan over again. His marriage to Agnes provided him with a new family and a new home.

Sir Charles Abraham Elton, Sir Arthur's father and Edmund's grandfather, had counted among his friends John Clare, Charles Lamb, Robert Southey and Samuel Taylor Coleridge. He had himself been a talented poet and had regularly contributed to *The Gentleman's Magazine* and *The British Critic*. His sister Julia had married the historian Henry Hallam whose *View of the State of Europe during the Middle Ages* had done much to promote the medievalism so rampant among nineteenth-century churchmen and architects. Hallam's son Arthur who had died young had been immortalised by Tennyson in the poem *In Memoriam*. In 1850 the poet had been a guest at Clevedon Court when he had visited Arthur Hallam's tomb. Thackeray, too, had been a visitor to the Court. He had fallen in love with Jane Octavia, Sir Charles Elton's youngest daughter, who, however, was married to Rev W. H. Brookfield, acknowledged as one of London's greatest dinner-table wits.

The literary interests of the family had been maintained by Sir Arthur Hallam Elton who had succeeded Sir Charles in 1853. He had written verses, political tracts and two novels. His daughter Agnes, according to Percy Thornton, had inherited 'his literary perception' and was herself 'an excellent judge of general literature'. Edmund, who had shown little intellectual aptitude during his education, must have found his uncle's and his wife's cultural conversation a little daunting.

At first, Edmund and Agnes seemed to have lived very much as would have been expected of a recently married couple of the landed gentry. They took a house in St George's Square, London, where on 23 May 1869, their first child was born, to be christened Ambrose. Edmund had decided that, in those years of agricultural depression due to cheap imports of wheat and beef from the New World, farming would not be a remunerative pursuit. Over the next three or four years the young Eltons lived much of the time in Devon. Edmund was largely engaged in activities befitting his station, such as hunting with the Devonshire and Somerset Staghounds and fishing. However, he also found time for other occupations rather less to be expected of the young heir to a baronetcy in mid-Victorian times. He made many competent watercolour sketches, including views of Launceston Castle, the King's Cave at Tintagel in Cornwall, Glastonbury Tor and Sidmouth (where he drew a charming portrait of Agnes sitting on the

Plate 2 Top left. Slipware vases. The landscape decoration on the vase in the centre is very unusual. Height of tallest 28.8 cm.

Plate 3 Bottom left. Slipware vases showing some of the different ground colours which Elton used. Height of tallest 19.8 cm.

Plate 4 Right. Slipware vases. The open-work neck of the right-hand vase indicates that it was made after 1900. Height of taller 33 cm.

beach). Otherwise, according to an account of his career given in *The Bristol Evening News* of March 27th, 1905, he was 'engaging in mechanics and art works of various kinds, such as wood-carving, painting on china, and designing furniture'. Of the last, no results seem to have survived. At Clevedon Court today there are three examples of Elton's wood carving which display not only considerable skill but also artistry and originality which are wholly unexpected from somebody without any formal training in art (fig. 10).

Although none of the china Elton painted at this time is known, it is this occupation that most deserves our attention in view of his later career. Elton had probably become aware that china decorating was a pastime that could

be enjoyed with the aid of only minimal equipment and materials when he had been at Cirencester. Church owned an earthenware tile that had been painted by William Morris in 1864 with a head of Geoffrey Chaucer. The decorations of the Grill Room at the Victoria & Albert Museum included tiles designed by E. J. Poynter and painted during the late 1860s by lady students at the South Kensington art school. This exercise had proved so successful that in 1871 Minton's opened their Art Pottery Studio in Kensington Gore, where instruction was given not only to art-school students but also to members of the public, most of them female and many of them from the upper echelons of society. It is unlikely that Elton attended the Art Pottery Studio, but he would certainly have been aware of the growing popularity of china painting. 'Nearly everybody took up pot-painting for a time,' wrote George W. Rhead, a Minton employee who worked at the Studio, '. . . It was indeed more than a craze; it became a positive fever.' When the Art Pottery Studio burnt down in 1875, two firms of china retailers, Howell & James in Regent Street and Phillips of Oxford Street, established studios on their premises where instruction was given. From 1876 Howell & James held annual exhibitions which became quite an event of the London season. Unfortunately, nothing is known of Elton's efforts in china painting at this time, nor is it at all clear what technical facilities he might have used.

In 1873 Sir Arthur was left a widower by

Fig. 10 Left. Carved wooden box made by Edmund Elton c. 1870.

Fig. 11 Right. The Great Hall, Clevedon Court, c. 1890. The vases on the mantelpiece are examples of Elton ware.

Plate 5 Top left. Slipware vases and jug. Height of tallest 23.2 cm. Jug dated 1882.

Plate 6 Bottom left. Slipware vessels. One jug features a spout in the form of a bird and the others its developing abstraction. Height of tallest 25.7 cm.

Plate 7 Right. Slipware jug and vases. The fish form of the spout and handle was a motif which was used by several West Country potters and which Elton employed to great advantage. Height of tallest 39.8 cm.

the death of Lady Rhoda Elton. This had two effects on Edmund Elton's life, apart from the grief he must have felt. The first direct consequence was that he and Agnes moved into Clevedon Court. The second indirect result was that he came into contact with one of the giants of Victorian architecture, William Butterfield. When Sir Arthur decided to build a church in Clevedon to the memory of his wife, he first called on the services of the architect John Sedding who had married a niece of his, Rose Tinling. Sedding, however, refused to accept the commission when he mistakenly perceived that Sir Arthur Elton wished to dictate in matters of architectural style. Butterfield must have been a lot more expensive; he was at that time at the top of his profession whereas Sedding was a comparative tyro. Butterfield was, however, the natural choice for a man of Sir Arthur Elton's ecclesiastical allegiance. Sir Arthur firmly belonged to that party in the Church of England which had been spawned by the Oxford Movement and was described as High Church or Catholic, and, by its Evangelical detractors, as Popish. To protect itself from Low Church harassment and to promote its cause the Catholic party had established the English Church Union during the 1860s, and both Sir Arthur and Edmund had soon become members. Butterfield had gained his reputation and consolidated his practice by obliging High Churchmen with decorated and ritualistic church buildings. At the time when Sir Arthur

Elton commissioned him to build St John's church in Clevedon Butterfield was working on Keble College chapel which was being paid for by William Gibbs, a banker and merchant, whose family was related to the Eltons by the marriage of George Louis Monck Gibbs to Laura Beatrice, Agnes's older sister.

Butterfield was entertained at Clevedon Court on more than one occasion while the church was being built from 1876 to 1878. Although by then Sir Arthur had married again and Edmond had moved his family to Firwood, a house close by, there must have been some occasions for talk between Butterfield and Edmond. Nor would it seem too speculative to assume that some at least of their conversations would have been taken up with the subject of church decoration. The floor and lower part of the walls in St John's were covered in ceramic tiles and the reredos was decorated in mosaic. In 1878 discussions were being held concerning designs for the stained glass windows. Sir Arthur and his second wife Bessie both took an active part, sometimes overruling Butterfield's ideas.

The same year there appeared a new periodical called *The Ecclesiastical Art Review*. The first issue, published in February, contained an article by the architect John Pollard Seddon on 'Decorative Processes in Ecclesiastical Art'. This was how it opened:

It seems to me that a very essential aim for a new journal devoted to Ecclesiastical Art should be to watch for and welcome every new development of

Fig. 12 Right. Sketch designs for altar candlesticks c. 1890.

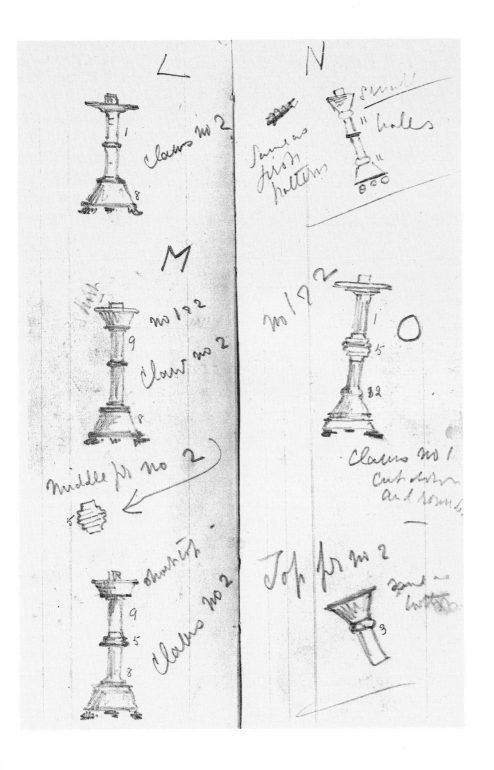

material or process of manufacture calculated to give to architects and artists greater facility for expression and design.

Seddon goes on to recommend the use of glass mosaics and stoneware, both of which he had used in churches that he had built himself. His article provoked some correspondence which was published in the March issue of the *Review*. A letter from 'J.L.B.' is worth quoting at length:

> ... most of the present attempts at tile decoration, especially in churches, are rather warnings of what to avoid than examples of what might be done ... But is not this the result of the abuse, and not the use, of our rich and varied clays? Could not better things be attempted than these? What has been done at [Butterfield's] All Saints, Margaret-street, is sufficient to show that far higher results may be attained, and that we have here in our midst a material which could be so altered and adapted that we should be enabled to use it with great advantage for church decoration –a material capable of being decorated in the highest and most artistic manner.

It was in this atmosphere of private discussion and public debate that Edmund Elton conceived the idea of making pottery mosaics for the decoration of churches. He mulled over the idea for several months before he perceived the means of its implementation. He was, he recalled thirty years

Plate 8 Left. Slipware vase (left); jar and cover (right) decorated with crackled lustre both c. 1905. Height of taller 58.9 cm.

Plate 9 Right. Pierced, double-walled vases decorated with crackled lustre. Height of taller 32.6 cm.

later, 'more or less interested in arts and manufacture', and visiting a local brickworks in December 1879 he decided to try making 'clay mosaics to be coloured and glazed for the decoration of church walls' (*Bristol Observer*, November 26th, 1910). It is ironic that having discovered the technical processes required he then, to all intents and purposes, gave up church decoration.

He completed and fired some panels of saints for a reredos, one of which was good enough to exhibit. But he then started making art pottery which, if not quite pagan, was entirely secular. However, John Ruskin had taught that any artistic creativity, if undertaken in the right spirit, was an act of worship, and it was in that spirit that Edmund Elton embarked on his career as a potter.

Fig. 13 Left. Pierced, double-walled vases and jugs in biscuit, 1901. Photograph reproduced in *Art Journal* 1901, p. 376.

Fig. 14 Left. Altar cross and candlesticks decorated with crackled lustre, in the church of SS Quiricus and Julietta, Tickenham. Height of cross 72 cm.

Fig. 15 Right. Altar cross, candlesticks and altar-table pillars in the church of SS Quiricus and Julietta, Tickenham. Height of cross 86 cm.

Plate 10 Top left. Vases, tyg and jug decorated with crackled lustre; vase second from the right with resist decoration. The tyg is an interesting combination of early English pottery form with decoration of oriental inspiration. Height of tallest 30.2 cm.

Plate 11 Bottom left. Jars, vases and tyg decorated with crackled lustre over variously coloured grounds. Height of tallest 26.3 cm.

Plate 12 Right. Vases decorated with crackled lustre, one with relief decoration (left), one with resist decoration (right). Height of taller 67.5 cm.

Fig. 16 Left. 'A country
baronet and two boot-
boys.' Left to right,
George Masters, Charlie
Neads, Sir Edmund Elton
c. 1888.

Chapter 2

The Pottery

Despite the misunderstanding which had led to Sedding's not building St John's, the architect remained on friendly terms with his mother-in-law's family. Edmund Elton may well have heard about the architect's meeting Ruskin in 1876, an encounter that had a profound effect on Sedding. The architect who was to be so instrumental in the development of the arts and crafts movement would surely have encouraged Elton to take up pottery, and his designs for embroidery, wallpapers and metalwork, usually based on floral motifs, must have been a source of inspiration to the aspiring potter.

Sedding, however, would have been no help in overcoming the myriad technical problems that beset Elton when he started out as a potter. In this respect, Professor Church

was better qualified to provide assistance. The article on Elton's pottery which Church published in *The Portfolio* towards the end of 1882 has a flavour of personal involvement when recounting Elton's technical setbacks and how they were overcome. However, when Church gave a series of lectures on 'Some points of contact between the scientific and artistic aspects of pottery and porcelain' at the Society of Arts during the winter of 1880–1881, he said: 'I shall not attempt to offer instruction in practical potting, of which I know far too little for my own satisfaction.' Perhaps Elton's plight had brought home to him his own limitations. But it had probably been under his former professor's guidance that Elton had, according to Church's article in *The Portfolio*, studied 'old examples and the

31

Plate 15 Below. Vessel decorated with crackled lustre. Height 22.3 cm.

Plate 16 Below. Slipware plaque, lustre decoration. Diameter 36.8 cm.

Plate 14 Below. Vases decorated with unusual crackled lustres. Height of taller 12.4 cm.

Plate 13 Left. Jugs and pierced stand decorated with crackled lustre. Height of tallest 27.4 cm.

Plate 17 Below. Slipware vases, lustre decoration. Elton began to use lustre decoration c. 1902, but at first it was only used as an embellishment to the slipware. Height of taller 32 cm.

literature of the subject'; not that there had been much literature to be studied, which offered practical advice or instruction.

The only written works that Elton is known to have consulted for technical assistance were the *Catalogue of Specimens in the Museum of Practical Geology* (1871) and a weekly magazine edited by J. Passmore Edwards called *English Mechanic*. Pasted into a book in which Elton kept notes on technical matters are some clippings from the *English Mechanic*. These are readers' queries and the replies which they elicited, and they only deal with quite rudimentary points. For instance: 'Can any reader inform me of a good transparent glaze not requiring more than ordinary heat for red ware?' Next week came the reply: 'All glazes require rather more than ordinary heat . . .', and there followed a recipe. Another reader's letter which Elton had cut out and pasted in his notebook gave details of 'a process of making bricks, tiles, &c., without burning'. The clippings are all from issues of the magazine that had been published in 1872, 1873 and 1875, suggesting that Elton had started to think of making pottery even then, probably when trying his hand at painting on china.

The *Catalogue of Specimens in the Museum of Practical Geology* by Trenham Reeks, the museum's curator, was more helpful. Elton's notebook contains a section headed 'Samples of lead glazes from Reeks'. The *Catalogue* contains formulae of many glazes and also gives the composition of many English clays,

Fig. 17 Left. Slipware plaque. Diameter 31.5 cm.

together with the name and address of their principal suppliers, some of which Elton copied in his notebook.

His visit to Pountney's Victoria Pottery in Bristol was, however, probably the most important part of Elton's education in ceramic technology. To be allowed to examine and measure an enamelling kiln there, reflected the privileges that rank bestowed. The Elton family had provided several Lord Mayors of Bristol and was connected by marriage to two of the wealthiest merchant families in the city. Mr Rogers, a solicitor who managed Pountney's at that time, having bought the pottery in partnership with another solicitor, Mr Johnston, in 1878, would have felt obliged to offer the Elton heir every possible assistance. Few other would-be potters could

Fig. 18 Right. Plate, painted decoration on commercial blank, c. 1880.

have hoped to have gained such unrestricted access to a working pottery. The arcana of the ceramics industry were jealously guarded.

What Elton saw at Pountney's may well have headed him in the direction of the kind of decorated pottery he was to make, once he had decided not to persevere with mosaic panels. A brief return that he made to painted pottery was not so much an aesthetic exercise as a technical experiment; he wanted to check the viability of colours he had developed on already fired blanks which were a known quantity (fig. 18). Thus he could confirm that it had been his clay body which had been faulty at that stage. The finest work that had been done at Pountney's had been a ware decorated with flowers minutely detailed in high relief. Edward Raby who had done most of the modelling on this ware had left Pountney's in

1864, but examples of the ware were still on display at the pottery in the 1880s. Elton decorated one of his vases, dated 1881, in a manner suggesting an attempt by a skilful beginner to imitate Raby's work (fig. 19). This pot, however, was exceptional; Elton quickly adopted a style of decoration in which flowers, birds, fish and insects were modelled in much lower relief and much less detail.

'The method of decoration,' wrote Church in his article in *The Portfolio*, 'characteristic of what is known as "slipware" commended itself to him, as possessing many technical advantages and promising good results from the artistic standpoint.' Part of the appeal of sixteenth- and seventeenth-century English slipware to Elton was its primitive quality. 'It was very clearly in his mind at this time,' wrote Charles Quentin in the *Art Journal* in 1901, 'that as the Pre-Raphaelites had discarded modern teaching in painting and all modern schools, he might do the same in pottery.' In 1883 Cosmo Monkhouse wrote of Elton in the *Magazine of Art*: 'He began, as he says, like an ancient Briton.' Church traced the genealogy of English slipware back to the Romano-British culture, and a bowl made by Elton in 1882 was decorated with a geometrical pattern of small blobs of slip, in the style of Romano-British pottery. In an article on old English slipware that Church wrote for *The Portfolio* in 1893, he commented on a piece that it was 'spontaneous and untaught, yet wholly congruous with the life of the day'. That the primitive

Plate 18 Top left.
Slipware vases, lustre
decoration c. 1902.
Height of tallest 33 cm.

Plate 19 Bottom left.
Slipware vases, lustre
decoration c. 1902.
Height of tallest
27.3 cm.

forms and decoration of old English pottery were also 'wholly congruous with the life of the late nineteenth century was established in 1883 when M.-L. Solon published *The Art of the Old English Potter*. The list of subscribers to this volume reads like a who's who of the modern decorative arts of that time; it included Edward C. Moore of Tiffany's, Louis Comfort Tiffany himself, Christian Herter the New York cabinetmaker, Charles E. Haviland the Limoges porcelain and stoneware manufacturer, Eugène Rousseau who designed pottery and glassware in Paris and Thomas Wardle whose factory at Leek dyed and printed textiles for William Morris.

A source of inspiration to most of these designers and manufacturers was Japanese art. Elton used floral and animal motifs in the decoration of his pottery that would appear to have been derived from Japanese ornament. He might have referred to the numerous illustrations in Thomas W. Cutler's *A Grammar of Japanese Ornament and Design* which was published in four separate parts from 1879 to 1880, but Professor Church could have provided him with a more direct experience of Japanese art. In 1873 Church had started collecting Japanese sword-guards made of iron, bronze or other metal alloys, sometimes in conjunction with silver and gold. The nature of the decoration of many sword-guards is suggested by Elton's work. The guards often combine relief decoration of flowers, insects or birds in silver or gold laid on a ground of bronze or some other alloy which has been incised with, for instance, reeds, clouds, water or a diaper pattern. As in the case of Elton's pottery, there are two levels of decoration in addition to the plane of the object itself. It is, however, flying in the face of Elton's own words to suggest that his decorative scheme was derived from metalwork. He maintained that the style of his decoration was governed by the nature of the clay vessel in front of him, and the tools he used. 'He has not sought,' wrote Cosmo Monkhouse in 1883, 'to impose upon his ware any preconceived ideas of decoration gathered from other branches of art.' If his decoration was inspired by Japanese sword-guards, that inspiration would have been of a nature described by A. H. Church in his 1893 account of old English slipware, particularly 'Toftware':

> The ultimate origin of these designs may perhaps be traceable to the coins or medals, or to the embroideries or the bookbinding of the day; but the homely potter, in translating the patterns before him into clay, has imparted to them an air of quaint simplicity which has a charm peculiarly its own.

Another aspect of Japanese influence on Elton is apparent in his handles, spouts and feet modelled as grotesque human figures or masks, animals, reptiles and fish. However, it is always difficult to decide whether or where a line should be drawn between Japanese and medieval European influence in respect of grotesque figures and masks. A specific instance of Oriental influence can, perhaps, be detected in one of Elton's decorative motifs. To act as feet on some vases he modelled figures of grotesque humans or animals (fig. 27 and colour plate 10), and although these vases were probably not made until twenty years later the idea for the feet may well have come from a Korean vase illustrated in the May 1887 issue of the *Magazine of Art*, the only art periodical known to have been taken by Elton. The more or less abstracted bird that Elton frequently made into the spout on a jug, or used as a handle on a lid (fig. 21, colour plates 6, 8, 13), was based on the pheasant, a common enough sight on the Clevedon estate where they were reared for shooting.

The *Magazine of Art* may also have been the source of the more elaborate shapes that Elton gave some of his pots. Vessels with several handles – an Elton speciality – were common in seventeenth-century English slipware, but jugs and pitchers with pro-truding spouts and overhead handles (fig. 23) probably relate to the pieces of peasant pottery from Mediterranean countries which were used as studio props by many Victorian painters and which frequently appear in their paintings. Such pots were featured in E. Munier's *At the Spring*, engraved in the *Magazine of Art* in 1886, and in Luke Fildes' *Venetians*, engraved in 1888. Other shapes that appeared in Elton's work were derived from Japanese ceramics, such as the gourd and seed-pod forms, and the pottery of Central and South America. Excavations of Pueblo settle-ments in New Mexico about 1880 and of Inca sites in Peru in 1886 revealed quantities of pottery, and examples were illustrated in periodicals such as the *Illustrated London News*.

As Edmund Elton developed an artistic style embracing elements of old English slipware and Japanese ornament, among other ingredients, at the same time he and George Masters were perfecting the processes of manufacture. This procedure hardly varied over the years, except when the crackle ware was made after 1902. Sir Edmund Elton's description of how both sorts of pottery were made, which he gave in 1910, is reprinted in Appendix I. But there were many disasters which befell the pottery over the years, and it would be wrong to think that there was ever anything like a production line turning out Elton-ware on a regular basis. Sir Edmund Elton's imagination was too adventurous for him ever to have been satisfied with what he knew he could make. He was always experi-menting, trying to achieve new effects. In a diary, which he started in January 1884 but only kept regularly up to September of that year (entries thereafter being frustratingly spasmodic), he wrote on February 23rd: 'Very busy pulling down kiln and making it larger, hope and trust it will succeed.' Another entry, for July 13th 1884, indicates the strange mixture of hope and despondency with which Elton regarded his work as a potter:

Pottery works fairly in order, but we have been through much trouble and

Fig. 19 Top right.
Slipware vases and jug.
Height of tallest
22.8 cm. These early
pots were probably all
made between 1880 and
1882; the vase second
from right is dated 1881.

Fig. 20 Bottom right.
Slipware vases, jug and
covered jar. The jug and
vase in the centre display
two contrasting forms
which Elton favoured.
Height of tallest
22.7 cm.

Fig. 21 Top left. Slipware pierced stand, covered jar, vase and jug. The mask on the jug could have been derived from either Japanese art or medieval sculpture. Height of tallest 24.2 cm.

Fig. 22 Bottom left. Slipware vases and jug. The vegetable form of the jug is an instance of Elton's borrowing a shape from Japanese pottery, as well as a style of decoration. Height of tallest 37.5 cm.

Fig. 23 Top right. Slipware teapots. The form of the second from the left has been borrowed from peasant pottery found in many Mediterranean countries; this source of pottery had become very popular amongst Victorian artists, who often featured examples in their paintings. Height of tallest 28.5 cm.

Fig. 24 Bottom right. Commemorative pieces. Left to right: Queen Victoria's Diamond Jubilee 1897, coronation of Edward VII 1902, Queen Victoria's Golden Jubilee 1887, General Roberts, General Kitchener. Height of tallest 23 cm.

use — looks so like RK — genetically interesting, the hands.

Fig. 25 Far left. Jack Flowers turning the wheel 1896.

Fig. 26 Left. Sir Edmund Elton decorating c. 1890.

Fig. 27 Top right. Vases, covered jar and jug decorated with crackled lustre. Height of tallest 35.5 cm.

Fig. 28 Bottom right. Vases and jug decorated with crackled lustre. These five vases demonstrate the remarkable diversity of Elton's artistic inspiration, and also his ability to adapt successfully a variety of stylistic traditions. Height of tallest 49.2 cm.

uneasiness with the ware, so many misfortunes that I feel sometimes that I must give it up. Still, I seem so near getting some splendid results I live in hopes of some day opening a kiln and finding its contents matchless! I can see such beautiful things in my mind's eye.

Elton's pottery received copious publicity almost immediately. It was not every day the heir to a baronetcy started making pots. A reporter from the popular magazine *All the Year Round* was quickly on the scene, and his lengthy article was published in November 1882. More critical and discerning accounts of Elton's endeavours followed, a concise but well-informed piece by A. H. Church appearing in the December 1882 issue of *The Portfolio*, and a longer, well-illustrated article by Cosmo Monkhouse being published in the *Magazine of Art* the following spring.

Elton at first called his ware 'Sunflower Pottery' but by the time that Church's article appeared at the end of 1882, the author had to report that the name had been changed to 'Elton Ware'. No reason was given; it may have been thought prudent in the light of the unremitting scorn with which *Punch* treated the Aesthetic Movement, and *Patience* had been produced the year before, making it hard to think of sunflowers without smirking. It was a pity that the name was abandoned (although it was used again occasionally years later); Elton had had some beautiful embossed writing paper made featuring the eponymous bloom (fig. 29).

A comprehensive list of the exhibitions where Elton's pottery was shown is given in Appendix II. Probably the most worthwhile exhibitions from the point of view of increasing trade outlets were the small display of Elton Ware which was shown at Howell & James's store in 1883, and his participation in the Chicago World's Fair of 1893. The presence of Elton's pottery at the annual exhibition of painting on china at Howell & James, a prestigious and well-attended event, would have alerted the leading London china retailers, many of whom subsequently ordered pottery from Sir Edmund. Apart from selling over £100 worth at the World's Fair of 1893 in Chicago, his display there attracted the attention of a Tiffany's buyer, and the New York store quickly became easily his best customer. Also as a result of his display at Chicago he had requests for examples of his work from museums in Stuttgart and Copenhagen. The director of the Stuttgart Museum asked him to 'yield some typical specimens of the Elton Ware to the Royal Museum on easy conditions'.

Elton once told a reporter from *The World* that his pottery was made by a 'country baronet and two boot-boys'. George Masters, having been inspanned at the pottery's very beginning, remained Sir Edmund's assistant until the end, becoming almost as much a friend as an employee (figs. 6, 16, 33, 35, 36). He seems to have done most of the throwing and to have been in attendance through most of the firings. Occasionally he decorated

Fig. 29 Top right.
Embossed device on
Sunflower Pottery
writing paper.

Fig. 30 Bottom right.
The pottery buildings at
Clevedon Court c. 1885.

pieces, which he signed with initials; his work was much cruder and less artistic than Sir Edmund's (fig. 31). He was awarded a medal for his work as a collaborator at the Franco-British Exhibition held at the White City in 1908, and he won a prize in the Turners' Company competition of 1914.

If Masters was a permanent 'boot-boy' the second one came and went. One was Charlie Neads (fig. 16), another was Jack Flowers (fig. 25), and a third was Henry Isgar. The last named was credited as an assistant in the catalogue of the Arts & Crafts Exhibition Society's 1889 show. None of them seems to have remained long at the pottery, nor do they seem to have made any significant contribution to the enterprise.

In 1882 the west wing of Clevedon Court was burnt down and most of the library was destroyed by fire. The catastrophe hastened the end of Sir Arthur Elton who died on October 14th, 1883. Edmund Elton succeeded; he was the eighth baronet. He and Agnes, their two boys, Ambrose and Bernard, and their three girls, Kathleen, Winifred and Angela, moved from Firwood back into Clevedon Court. In addition to his own interests and occupations, Sir Edmund Elton was now also saddled with the affairs of the estate and the duties that came with the title. He was on the bench and a prominent figure in local government. He served as High Sheriff of Somerset from 1894 to 1895. He was involved in several philanthropic organisations and was an officer of many sports clubs in Clevedon. He served in the Volunteers which he often found irksome. 'Drills Thursdays and Tuesdays,' he noted in his diary on January 17th, 1884, 'an awful bore!!!' The Fire Brigade, however, he enjoyed. It was formed in 1883 and Sir Edmund led it conscientiously and gallantly until 1910, not even baulking at a call to Naich House in Portishead on Christmas Day, 1902.

Elton always showed great civic pride and was happy to mark Queen Victoria's Diamond Jubilee in 1897 by presenting a clock tower to the town of Clevedon. It was decorated with two courses of tiles which showed the birds of the air, the beasts of the field and the fishes under the sea. Apparently their manufacture

Fig. 31 Left. Slipware jug decorated with lustre, signed 'G.F.M.' for George Masters. Height 20 cm.

Fig. 32 Right. The Clevedon Fire Brigade c. 1900. Sir Edmund Elton is at the reins; Alonzo Dawes, secretary, is standing on the left with his hand tucked into his coat.

did not go as smoothly as it might have, and the tower was not ready for its official presentation until 1898.

Sir Edmund had an attractive character. He was capable rather than clever, as we have seen, and his humour was comic rather than witty. He enjoyed amateur theatricals, and used to give solo performances after dinner, acting out some comic situation. One evening, Lord Arthur Hervey, Bishop of Bath and Wells, had been a dinner guest at Clevedon Court, when Sir Arthur had still been living. After the meal, Edmund was invited to do one of his comic turns; he chose 'The Visit to the Dentist'. Sir Arthur wondered why an uneasy silence had fallen over his guest, and, looking in his direction, was horrified to see all the signs on the prelate's countenance of a recent mass extraction. Edmund had winged another Bishop of Bath and Wells!

Strong in Sir Edmund's emotional make-up was that compassion bordering on sentimentality which was so common among the Victorian upper classes. He was very moved by a lecturer who spoke against the use of vivisection in the study of anatomy and he remonstrated with his diary: 'There are girls even, it seems, at Girton College near Oxford [sic] who are indulging with pleasure in the diabolical study!' Later the same year his diary reveals him as having a more genuine pity for dumb animals. After shooting a stag with horns of eleven points, he wrote: '. . . there is much that is painful and butcherly about this sport. The stag is such a noble specimen of

God's creation.' But unlike most Victorian gentleman who would have happily hung a copy of 'The Monarch of the Glen' on their dining-room wall but would nevertheless have gone on slaughtering stags with alacrity, Sir Edmund was true to his conviction and gave up the sport. He satisfied his blood-lust in salmon-fishing, and took his exercise by going on long bicycle rides.

In 1900, Sir Edmund Elton showed his pottery at the Universal Exhibition in Paris. His methods of production were still far from faultless. 'Even as recently as last year,' wrote Charles Quentin in the *Art Journal* in 1901, 'Sir Edmund met with a trying failure. Some work being specially prepared for the Paris Exhibition became, through accident, unfit to exhibit, and the few examples he sent only won for him a bronze medal . . .' It is not known for certain whether Sir Edmund visited the Exhibition himself, but the direction that his work took in the following years would suggest that he was fully informed about the other pottery exhibits. In 1901 Charles Quentin noted 'some very recent work done at Clevedon Court' which had pierced decoration, and one of the most talked-about displays of pottery at the Paris Exhibition had been the open-work porcelain shown by the Swedish firm of Rörstrand.

'In 1902, a new departure was made,' Sir Edmund said in 1910, 'when I began to introduce gold and platinum in decoration.' The Rookwood Pottery of Cincinnati, Ohio, had exhibited at Paris vases decorated by the

Fig. 33 Right. The Clock Tower, Clevedon, nearing completion 1898. Sir Edmund Elton and George Masters are the left-hand pair standing on the scaffolding.

Japanese artist R. Ito with designs part of which were covered by the electro-deposit process with silver. Some glassware shown by Loetz at Paris was decorated by the same process. The effect achieved by Elton with his slipware vases with areas covered in gold or platinum lustre is very similar to that of the Loetz and Rookwood decoration. Like those wares, too, Elton's metallic decoration had a very shiny, mirror-like appearance, and it was in the course of experiments made to tone down this brilliant shine that Sir Edmund first produced his crackled lustre effects.

Lewis F. Day, writing on 'Modern Pottery at the Paris Exhibition' in the *Art Journal*, declared:

> The recent reaction of prejudice against precise and mechanical execution, and the bias of a section of the public towards whatever is accidental in result, have had a very marked effect upon the practice of the potter.

He went on to describe in rather disparaging tones the crystalline and crackled glazes which were so widely featured at the Paris Exhibition. Edmund Elton would have been delighted when in 1902, he discovered his crackled lustre effect, and dismayed when two years later there occurred what he dubbed 'the disease'. There is a notebook at Clevedon Court which contains his account of the unremitting warfare that he and George Masters waged against the difficulties of achieving the desired effects. In the autumn of 1904 the silver and platinum lustres started coming out of the kiln black. Sir Edmund and George were baffled. 'We then sent a piece of the black up to Stoke on Trent for advice.' Various experts offered a range of erroneous opinions. 'Before we had received this joint report of ceramic wiseacres, we found the *cause* ourselves, although we still do not know the *reason.*'

The notebook continues to record troubles as well as successes. During 1905, 1906 and 1907 results seem to have been largely satisfactory, and this may have had something to do with the fact that A. H. Church visited Clevedon those years, although there is no mention of him in the notebook. In 1909 misfortune struck again. Reporting a firing in April Elton wrote: 'Dishes and plaques all right, the rest all wrong.' He reckoned he knew the problem:

Fig. 34 Left. Page from one of Sir Edmund's notebooks, referring to experiments with crackled lustre.

Fig. 35 Right. George Masters throwing 1896.

Fig. 36 Far right. Sir Edmund Elton and George Masters c. 1890.

50

Potters Wheel 189

'Think something comes out of the fireclay to cause the mischief – if this is not the case *I am at my wits end.*' Matters, however, improved. The notebook explains how in 1911 the lustres with resist decoration came about (colour plates 10, 12). From a lustre firing, some pieces

> were inferior, so I tried the following. Paint over copper with pattern in spirit varnish; then paint over with fluoric acid till glaze was eaten into and copper lustre destroyed where not covered with spirit varnish, thus showing coloured body. Then either leave it so or re-lustre – or gild, or platinum. This will leave bright patterns on dead ground.

An entry towards the end of the notebook reads: 'Since January 1912 have tried countless experiments with varying results . . .'

At the outbreak of the First World War in 1914 Sir Edmund was sixty eight years old. For a number of years he had not been well. His ailment, which never seems to have been identified, first appeared in 1902, and its advent was sufficiently savage for him to resign that year from the Volunteers, and to make a gift of a collection of his pottery to the County Museum at Taunton. In April 1903, a relative wrote to Lady Agnes: 'He thinks his body is an inexhaustible machine from which he can draw any amount of work – pottery – bicycling – fire brigade – fishing – church work – E[nglish] C[hurch] U[nion].' He recovered sufficiently to work hard again at the pottery, as we have seen, but gradually the spring wound down.

He died on July 17th 1920 and was buried in All Saints churchyard on July 28th (fig. 37). His elder son, Ambrose, succeeded him. Sir Ambrose tried to keep the pottery going. George Masters was in too much pain to help, and he died on June 4th 1921; on his headstone is inscribed: 'For 43 years the friend and collaborator of the late Sir Edmund Elton Bt.' The potter W. F. Holland came to Clevedon to assist Sir Ambrose, but he was not really interested in Sir Edmund's work and soon set up his own pottery.

In the 1880s Sir Edmund had given a piece of his pottery to Sir Philip Cunliffe Owen, the director of the South Kensington Museum. Acknowledging the gift Sir Philip wrote:

> I look at the particular vase you gave me with a good deal of pleasure and think it will be one day looked upon as one of the wonderful examples of the age when men like yourself, instead of spending their time in a lawn-tennis field, are willing to go through the fire necessary to produce such work as you have presented me with.

Let him speak for us all!

Fig. 37 Right. Sir Edmund Elton's coffin borne by members of the Clevedon Fire Brigade into All Saints church, July 28th, 1920.

THE STORY OF ELTON WARE.

(Gathered from " The Magazine of Art," " The Portfolio," Art Journal, &c.)

Manufactured and designed by Sir E. H. ELTON, at

THE SUNFLOWER POTTERY,

CLEVEDON, Somerset.

AGENTS FOR ELTON WARE:

CHALLICOM & CO.,

10 & 12, HILL ROAD, CLEVEDON.

Fig. 38 Left. Brochure issued by Challicom & Co, Clevedon agents for Sir Edmund Elton's pottery c. 1910.

Fig. 39 Right. Elton ware
publicity material
c. 1890.

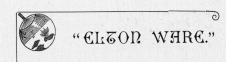

"ELTON WARE."

Elton Ware is manufactured and
designed by Sir E. H. ELTON, Bart.,
at the Sunflower Pottery, Clevedon,
Somerset. It is the only Art Pottery
produced in Somerset, and has been
awarded nine Gold and two Silver
Medals at various Exhibitions, including Edinburgh, Brussels, Antwerp,
Atlanta, California, Tasmania, and
Jamaica.

Appendix I

*Sir Edmund Elton's account of the processes by which his pottery was
made, from a lecture he gave to the Somersetshire Archaeological and
Natural History Society, printed in the Society's Proceedings, LVI (1910),
Part II, pp 31–37.*

The general lines of the process in those early days for the coloured ware
was as follows – though many changes in detail have been made, and disasters
from various causes have not been unfrequent. The body of "Elton Ware" was
then, as now, principally formed of the ordinary red brick-clay of the district,
mixed with white, or with Rockingham. The method of manufacture differs
little from that used by our Somerset forefathers in forming their pitchers and
posset-cups, which are found in the neighbourhood to-day. First the clays are
mixed with water to about the consistency of cream, and then passed through
fine sieves of wire-lawn, after which the moisture is driven off by heat, dug out,
and beaten together till the mass is homogeneous. It is now ready for the
thrower. The piece to be decorated is formed entirely on the wheel, and
subsequently handled or spouted and finished by hand, no turning being
resorted to. After a period of drying, the pattern is cut with a suitable wooden
tool, and is coated entirely with coloured clays about as thick as an egg-shell,
when a further period of drying has to be undergone. The spaces between the
cut lines is then filled with clay-slips which have been coloured by the

admixture of various oxides. These are applied rather thick, leaving the pattern in slight relief.

Then comes the finishing, which may be very simple or very elaborate, and consists of further raising with thick clay paste. Further effects may be produced by modelling or by incised lines. Nothing is now required but drying and firing, but this final operation is no easy task. First it is burnt at a low heat, say 850 centigrade, and when cool taken from the kiln and coated with a clear uncoloured plumbic glaze. It is then returned to the kiln and fired to the highest possible heat, say 1050 or 1100 centigrade. Success now depends on many things, and I can only say that I have found that small kilns cannot as a rule be depended upon. If the temperature has not been too high or too low – if the fumes of combustion have not entered the saggers – if no sand has fallen on the glaze – if no bubbling of the glaze has occurred – if the atmosphere has neither been too reduced nor too oxidising – well, then the best quality of "Elton Ware" may be expected.

An enamelling kiln was first used, now a saggar-kiln has taken its place; that is the only difference between now and then; and early specimens of "Elton Ware" may be found which do not compare unfavourably with those of 1910. In fact there are fine colours with effects which we have lost the art of producing, and as an example of the sort of thing, I may say that about eight years ago there was a very uncommon crimson red, which we are now unable to produce with any certainty. I myself have only one perfect specimen of this red.

In 1902, a new departure was made, when I began to introduce gold and platinum in decoration. Gilding was easy enough, but the crux in my mind was how to avoid the vulgarity so easily introduced with gold. To avoid this, a series of experiments with precious metals were embarked upon, but some time elapsed before anything with promise or originality rewarded our efforts. One day I noticed a curious appearance, where some gold overlapped the platinum, which seemed likely to give unique and beautiful results if they could be obtained with certainty. This at first looked easy, and several other effects were also evolved. Four in particular struck me as worth working out on a larger scale, namely, "blue platinum crackle", "gold crackle", "bright platinum crackle", and "fiery platinum", so called because of the frosted gold crackle super-imposed on the "platinum crackle".

But, as if to rebuke presumption, troubles now began which took years to overcome. At first the body was very low-fired, and glazed with a very soft glaze, also very low-fired. This caused the ware not to be watertight; also white specks to appear on the glaze through under-firing. Only two specimens of "blue platinum crackle" survived out of the many pieces made, and the process was discontinued owing to the accurate temperature required involving too much uncertainty. "Gold crackle" shared the same fate owing to the same reason. "Bright platinum crackle" and "fiery platinum" were good from an artistic point of view, but I deemed it essential to produce it with a high-fired watertight body. This, however, started a fresh crop of difficulties; the high heat destroyed the regularity of the crackle. The platinum began to take on a blackish hue, and the "fiery platinum" became inferior and lost its brilliance, though several new effects were accidently produced, the most curious of them being two or three pieces of "gold crackle", which, when removed from the kiln, resembled copper, but gold was deposited on the edge of the crackles. The effect was curious and beautiful, but its reproduction has hitherto been found impossible, though attempted again and again. I have taken expert opinion, but can find no explanation of the mystery. It is only within the last few months that the metallic work has once more been produced with fairly certain results.

Appendix II

Exhibitions where Elton Ware was shown:–

1883	Bristol	Building Trades & Manufacturers Exhibition
	Bath	Bath & West
	London	Howell & James
1884	London	International Health Exhibition
	Bristol	Industrial Exhibition
1885	Taunton	Art, Science and Industrial Exhibition
	London	Howell & James
1889	London	Arts & Crafts Exhibition Society
1890	Newton Abbot	Cottage Art Schools Exhibition
	Plymouth	Western Counties Exhibition
	Edinburgh	International Electric Exhibition
	London	Arts & Crafts Exhibition Society

1891	Sheffield	Industrial Exhibition
	Derby	Midlands Counties Industrial Exhibition
	Wolverhampton	Midland Counties Trade Exhibition
	Kingston, Jamaica	International Exhibition
	Tasmania	International Exhibition
1893	Bristol	Industrial and Fine Art Exhibition
	Chicago	World's Fair
1894	San Francisco	Midwinter International Exposition
	Antwerp	Exposition Universelle
1895	Atlanta, Ga.	Cotton States and International Exposition
1897	Brussels	Exposition Universelle
1900	Bath	Century Exhibition of Arts, Industries and Inventions
	Paris	Exposition Universelle
1903	London	Arts & Crafts Exhibition Society
1904	St Louis	Louisiana Purchase Exposition
1905	Liège	Exposition Universelle
	Glasgow	People's Palace
1906	Milan	Esposizione Internazionale
	London	Arts & Crafts Exhibition Society
1908	London	Franco-British Exhibition
1910	London	Arts & Crafts Exhibition Society
1912	London	Arts & Crafts Exhibition Society
1913	Ghent	Exposition Universelle
1916	London	Arts & Crafts Exhibition Society

Appendix III

Stockists

Bath	F. Knight & Son	Exeter	Wipple
Bristol	J. Bell & Son	London	Art Furnishers Alliance
Chicago	Burley & Company		W. T. Bennett & Co
Clevedon	Challicom & Co		T. Goode & Co
	Lovegrove		Howell & James
Clifton	Catcheside	New York	Tiffany's
	Mackenzie	Taunton	Vile & Son

Fig. 40 Top right. Rare early marks. Left to right: 'E' incised, with 2 dots 'ELTON' impressed and 'Clevedon 1881' painted, 'Elton Clevedon' painted.

Fig. 41 Bottom right. Left to right: 'G.F.M.' for George Masters painted, 'E.H.Elton 1882' painted, standard mark 'Elton' painted. (Wares produced after Sir Edmund's death in 1920 were marked with a painted 'X' after the name).